Hands On

–A Rockin' Rhythmic Romp–

30 pieces with hand percussion for Grades 3 through Middle School

Jim Solomon
Foreword by Susan J. Jones

©2006 Alfred Publishing Co., Inc.
16320 Roscoe Blvd., Suite 100
P.O. Box 10003
Van Nuys, CA 91410-0003
All rights reserved. Printed in USA.

ISBN: 0-7390-4233-5
ISBN-13: 978-0-7390-4233-5

TABLE OF CONTENTS

The Pieces	Grade Level	
Annie Ate Jam	3rd–4th Grade	10
See a Pin	3rd–4th Grade	11
Charlie, Charlie in the Tub	3rd–4th Grade	12
Ice Cream	3rd–4th Grade	13
Pairs or Pears	3rd–4th Grade	14
Mister East Gave a Feast	3rd–4th Grade	15
Once a Year	3rd–5th Grade	16
Nellie Bligh	3rd–5th Grade	17
Big Turtle Sat	4th–5th Grade	18
Sleeper's Song	4th–5th Grade	19
Rain, Rain Canon	4th–5th Grade	20
Jack & Jill		
Version 1	4th–5th Grade	21
Version 2	5th Grade Special Group–Middle School	21
Peter White	4th–5th Grade	22
Once I Caught a Fish Alive	4th–5th Grade	23
See the Elephant Jump the Fence	4th–5th Grade	24
Christmas Is Coming	4th/5th Chorus–Middle School	25
Thump, Thump	4th–Middle School	26
The Bob	4th–Adult	28
From Wibbleton to Wobbleton	5th–Middle School	30
A Sieve	5th–Middle School	31
Poly 2 with 3	5th–Middle School	32
Eastside, Westside	5th–Middle School	34
Alligator Bongo, Alligator Drum	5th–Middle School	36
Confusion	5th–Middle School	37
Totally Chickenish	5th Grade Special Group–Middle School	38
Jungle	5th Grade Special Group–Middle School	40
Lost at "C" Rondo	5th Grade Special Group–Middle School	42
Ashes to Ashes	5th Special Group–Middle & High School	44
Butterfly (with Soprano Recorder)	5th–Middle School	45
Brisa Cambiando (with Soprano Recorder)	5th–Middle School	46

FOREWORD
by Susan J. Jones

Music's role in providing pleasure in our lives and enrichment in our culture has rarely been questioned. For years we've known that music can instantaneously alter one's mood—that hedonistic pleasures wrought by music keep us listening to the songs, buying CDs, and attending musical performances. But is that all music does, create a *mood?* Is it fair to consider music a frill, an add-on that deserves first consideration for cuts when the education budget is tight?

In the past twenty years, music and rhythm have taken on new importance as educators recognize that human intelligence extends beyond verbal or math skills. With Howard Gardner's *Theory of Mulitple Intelligences* and understanding of the "facets" of intelligence, we know musical skill may indeed be another manifestation of intelligence, communication and understanding. But the twenty-first century is opening with recognition that music might be more; it might serve as a means to improve brain wiring and hence, brain function. It *might be a tool to maximize learning.* That is, after all, the goal of educators: not simply to promote their disciplines, but to produce empowered and capable young people prepared to take on the challenges of life. Music is a vehicle for accomplishing just that.

Music enhances reasoning abilities at any age. Most educators are familiar with Fran Raucher's "Mozart Effect," which found that college students listening to Mozart improved their test performances. But research has also found that parts of the brain that coordinate physical movement (such as those necessary for playing percussion instruments) also coordinate the sequencing of thoughts and non-verbal creativity. The prefrontal and frontal regions of the cortical brain guide the motor cortex; so the brain circuits used to order, sequence, and time a *physical* act are the same as those that order, sequence, and time mental acts. Cognitive (thinking) and physical functions share parts of the same brain systems. Wiring the brain for higher level thinking, then, relates to wiring the brain for sequenced physical movement. It should come as no surprise that youngsters benefit from musical training, and that long-term boosts in cognitive skills after exposure to musical training are real. Studies suggest a connection between activity and levels of alertness, mental function, and learning. Spatial intelligence appears to improve when musical training is provided for children, allowing brains to form mental images and recognize variations in objects. Those are the skills needed by mathematicians, architects, engineers, and astronomers.

This book contains dozens of percussion pieces that utilize components of sound instruction for properly wiring brains to learn. *Hands On* musical tasks incorporate:

Movement: encourages young people to exercise large muscles and build fine motor skills, which strengthens motor synapses in the frontal lobe of the neo-cortex. It is these brain regions that manage mental behaviors, including attention and problem solving.

Rhythm and spatial intelligence: as a way to improve the mastery of other disciplines (math, science, language/reading, physical education).

Activity and exercise: to increase blood flow to the brain, allowing more oxygen and glucose for optimum brain function, and release endorphins, which positively impact mood.

Thought and attention: which is constructed not just out of perceiving objects, but also out of physical activities with them. Listening skills are developed with fast-paced, explicit instruction.

Cross lateral and gross motor movement: through the manipulation of instruments. The striking pattern of the drums and keyboard instruments develop the brain connections neccesary for the collaboration of the brain and body for expression and movement.

Pleasure and the creation of mood: have a primary component: emotion. Because emotion encodes all long-term memory, music can be a positive factor in learning. It is also effective at reaching at-risk or unmotivated students.

Chunking: content and skills in manageable units (such as lyrics or phrases) facilitates learning; especially for kinesthetic and tactile learners and children with limited memory space. Each musical unit exists as a single entity, making it much easier to plant and retrieve new memory.

Communication: music is a carrier of meaning for the student who needs an expressive outlet. It is a transmitter of culture and cross-cultural understanding, as well. Social Studies or Humanities, anyone?

As valuable as sound music instruction is, however, it is not universally available in our schools. Only small percentages of students join bands, orchestras or choruses, and usually not until the middle grades or later. Yet *all* students benefit from active participation in music making. How can we provide music's benefits in a way that is practical, powerful and exciting to students?

Several years ago I was fortunate to observe the author of *Hands On*, Jim Solomon, using percussion selections in his classroom. My visits began out of recognition of Jim's enthusiasm for teaching—but I soon discovered a classroom filled with activities that are engaging, purposeful, and productive for each child. It was magic.

Children love the process because the process honors the way children are captivated and the way the brain learns. Novelty, stimulation, and challenge engage each child with ever-present combinations of physical participation, choraling and rhythm. In Solomon's activities students play instruments, master catchy lyrics and collaborate with neighbors. But woven throughout are much-needed rituals: the rules, examples and demonstrations of performance possibilities or behavior limitations that establish rigid parameters to give clear guidance for safe and acceptable behavior. Students *know* the expectations.

Yet within the rigidity that guides proper behavior exist opportunities for choice, long known as an intrinsic motivator. Students are encouraged to improvise rhythms and movement: an invitation to risk-taking within a safe arena. Teacher-directed, with student choice—a challenge for each child to create a performance that meets established criteria. Solomon rewards divergent thinking; he expects problem solving. Problem solving! Higher level thinking skills develop as youngsters form solutions to meet criteria for a musical performance. Throughout it all, students are exposed to and required to identify patterns—a strategy that translates into categorizing and classifying skills useful in academic subjects such as math, science and language.

All, but particularly struggling students, benefit from such adult interest in their creativity; and percussion pieces provide an outlet for creative expression. They become part of a whole, bigger than themselves. Personal accomplishment is certainly important, but it is not just *my* answer or *my* performance—it is OURS. No one fails because all produce. No one is left out because all participate. Lessons are experiential and active, never passive. Even when sitting, youngsters are involved in a hands-on way, in their own world of sound and rhythm. So every activity creates a classroom of co-joined participants, not a group of spectators or solo performers. Each individual effort is integral to the final kid-generated performances.

These lessons are contagious. One experience, and the students will beg for more of the fun, the excitement, and the raucous sound! Even the most reluctant student can't help but find joy while experiencing music's relationship to mathematics, or weaving academic content like parts of speech into humorous lyrics. Active, whole-brain processing is, after all, more effective than reflective tasks for 67% of all the population, as memory circuits expand to include a multitude of brain regions.

Notice the process sequence for *Hands On* lessons:

1. Grab attention and engage students.

2. Impart understanding with the "big picture:" rich instruction; invitations to risk taking and novel approaches; strategies for problem solving.

3. Provide demonstrations and model process so students fully understand expectations, receive consistent rules and recognize rituals.

4. Provide practice.

5. Demand evaluation with objective criteria. (ex: *Who saw something good happen? What did you see? What could we do to make it a little better?*)

6. Repeat and rehearse to achieve mastery of the strategy.

7. Invite creativity and improvisation within the activity structure.

Every learning style is honored through the mixing of words, symbols, sound, gesture, body language, and visuals. Constant changes of state maintain learner attention with seamless, quick-paced transitions from one activity to the next. The whole brain-body is honored!

Hands On will serve as a guide and resource for not only music teachers, but also regular classroom teachers on the elementary and middle school level who find themselves responsible for or interested in incorporating music into their regular curriculum. Enjoy this treasure!

Susan J. Jones is a leading expert on instruction and student achievement and author of *Blueprint for Student Success: A Guide to Research-Based Teaching Practices K-12*, and *Backstage Pass for Trainers, Presenters, and Public Speakers*. She can be contacted at **sjjones@aug.com**.

INTRODUCTION

Hands On is a collection of thirty pieces with hand percussion instruments for grades 3 through middle school.

Hands On is also an attitude toward music education. Students in elementary school need tangible, physical experience to make knowledge meaningful. Students in middle school need tangible, physical experience to make knowledge relevant. For concrete and relevant learning, teachers must take an active music-making approach with children. Students learn through dynamic, *Hands On* music-making.

There is variety in this collection. Some pieces are pure conga jams, others are timbre studies to open the ears to a variety of percussion. Two pieces with recorder are included at the end. There are five $\frac{6}{8}$ pieces and one polymetric.

The pieces are grouped by approximate grade level. Keep in mind that the difficulty level can be radically altered by addition or deletion of parts. Feel free to do so!

Make the music your own! Have students create movement for the pieces. Add vocal sound effects. Feel free to adapt them to your students or have your students adapt them.

Why Percussion Ensemble?

Percussion ensemble (as well as Orff and recorder ensemble) develops musicianship in an extraordinary manner. Musicianship involves knowledge, skill and artistic sensitivity in performing music. A brief look illustrates a few of the ways that percussion ensemble builds musicianship:

1) Knowledge building through: work with Form (the structure of music); reinforcement of notation reading skills in learning the parts; understanding the problems/difficulties to be solved in each ensemble; understanding the social context of ensemble; learning the cultural context when appropriate.

2) Skill building through: playing parts with correct technique; learning to perform parts accurately; fitting the parts into the total ensemble (building independence); improvising.

3) Artistic Sensitivity through: playing within the context, i.e., fitting parts into the whole while following the plan of the group regarding tempo, dynamics and Form; keeping the parts synchronized throughout (focus).

Including improvisation fosters musicianship in a prodigious manner, as improvising requires skill to perform individually as well as the sensitivity to fit the improvisation into the ensemble.

The social benefit of percussion ensemble is immediate and powerful. It provides a dynamic tool to motivate our students to work together to achieve a sound that is far greater than the individual. All must play their individual parts accurately for the whole to succeed. The players receive immediate payback in fascinating, compelling sound when they perform their parts accurately. The self-discipline required to play the parts correctly gives immediate positive results.

Percussion ensemble provides a powerful motivational venue. Rhythm surrounds us. It springs from the movement of the earth. It's in the rhythm of our breathing, in the beating of our hearts. It touches us on a profound level.

Congas/Tubanos

The conga drum, featured in many of the pieces, is a user-friendly instrument that both students and teachers can play with great success by utilizing two strokes, the Bass (**B**) and the Tone (**T**):

"Bass" (**B**) = A powerful low pitched accent. Drive the palm into the center of the drum. The bass is played by either hand.

"Tone" (**T**) = The drum should ring out with a full sound; hit edge of drum head with the top edge of the palm. The hand should be flat and relaxed. This is done with either hand.

No congas? No tubanos? Use empty five-gallon water jugs. Turn them upside down, grab them between your knees and play the Basses and Tones like you would a conga. Call your local water company and ask about acquiring these.

The Teaching Process—A Few Basics

Directed Listening! Ask a question first or give the students an activity to perform before they hear the material each time! Set "The Hook." The hearing process must be interesting, even fascinating/involving/specific/instructive.

Elementary and middle school students are capable of playing very sophisticated rhythms. A critical element in the teaching process for the most difficult parts is to have the students meaningfully involved while they hear the rhythms repeatedly before they are asked to play them.

Movement is critical to students' learning. Include dance or movement that the students or you create as often as possible. Tell students, "Movement (Dance) makes you better at sports. It improves your timing and coordination."

The Brain keeps learning through Ritual, Novelty and Challenge. Design your room and your lessons so there are familiar procedures, a variety of materials, and constant challenge. Emotion has the greatest impact on memory—pick motivating material and utilize multimodal teaching techniques.

Instrument Parts: there are many, many techniques; one tried-and-true process is "Speech to Body Percussion to Instruments."

Conga/Tubano parts: highlight accents (Basses) first, as well as the most difficult rhythmic spots.

Improvisation, in order of complexity:

1) with the beat
2) "addition"
3) "subtraction"
4) variation
5) overlapping

Another excellent technique is for the students to choose model words to help guide their improvisations.

Recorder: there are many, many techniques; one tried-and-true process is to sing note names while moving fingers (after they have heard the melody enough through directed listening).

Modeling: 1. "Teacher talk" sometimes helps, but teacher demonstration is much better.
2. Student/teacher demonstration is far better than teacher alone.
3. Student/student demonstration while teacher talks it through is excellent.
4. Student/student demonstration while students talk it through with teacher guidance is the best.

The moral of this story is, "Get students involved in demonstrating parts to be learned!" This can be done by the teacher doing a quick demonstration, then having a class member pick other class members to come up and demonstrate.

Difficult parts: highlight them early in the teaching process. Sometimes it is best to teach these first. If students are struggling with a part you think they can get, challenge them! "We need <u>one</u> person who can do this! Who thinks they can?" Then call on one volunteer to try it. (When necessary, you play it with them.) If he/she gets it, say, "We have one! Do we have two?" Have another try, etc. When someone doesn't get it, compliment them for their excellent effort. "Good try! I'm proud of you!"

Visuals (charts, overheads, notation, etc.): use whenever possible to reinforce the learning. More than 65% of the population are primarily visual learners.

Older students: it is sometimes best to "go through the back door." If you are teaching a rhythm based on a nursery rhyme, instead of telling them the rhyme first, play the rhythm on the lead instrument after asking a question about what to look for as you perform it. Get them hooked by hearing the rhythm, then say that it comes from a rhyme that will help them learn the rhythm very quickly.

Which students get to pick instruments first when you start to practice the parts? This is an important fairness issue. Use a class list notebook. List the students by their seating order (my students have assigned spots in alphabetical order). Pick a student to have the first turn on the first day by having a member of the class give you a random number. Count down the class list that number and that student gets to go first. Check his/her name off. From that point on follow your list to pick the next students who get to go first. Suppose out of fifteen instruments, you have three that everyone considers to be the favorites. In that case, the first three students chosen are checked off. Then the next class starts with the next three students going first. In this way, the first turn rotation moves through the class. It moves slowly, but the students know it is fair.

Suppose you only have ten instruments. The first ten students fill up all the spots, one student per instrument, then the next ten line up behind the first ten, etc., until all students are lined up behind an instrument. After the first ten get to practice a part, they go to the back of their line and the next ten get a turn. Have short turns to work on each part so the students don't lose interest.

Humor energizes us! Use it unexpectedly and it will be a powerful teaching tool to raise the students' focus.

Starting points for pieces (includes the full variety of an elementary classroom): speech first/rhythm first/ dance-movement first/instruments first/song first/improvisation first/notation first. Variety in our teaching (novelty) is essential, so we must be prepared to use different starting points. These can overlap.

The Rotating Circle—An exceptional practice technique! We are stimulated by variety, by novelty. After the basic parts of an ensemble are taught, set up a circle of the instruments being used. Include enough instruments for the whole class, or pair up two or three students at each instrument. Vary the order of the instruments, i.e., drum/maracas/guiro/cowbell/etc. Each student plays the part for that instrument in the ensemble, then rotates to the next instrument, where they will play a different part. Give them 8 or 16 beats to rotate to the next instrument. Substitute instruments if you don't have enough, i.e., sticks for claves, five-gallon water jugs for congas, etc.

Always FOCUS ON THE GROOVE!

Form

Play with it. Have students create their own. Depending on the piece, make use of a variety of the following:

> Introductions
> Layering in as an Introduction
> Interludes
> **A**, **B**, **C**, etc. sections
> Improvisation sections
> Additive ensembles
> Fake endings (all stop for eight beats then begin again)
> Accelerando at the end
> Fade outs
> Fade outs with one instrument continuing then layering the instruments back in
> "Group solos" (one group continues playing its part while all the others stop)

Having students devise the form enables them to grasp how music is structured, how it is put together. It also gives them ownership of the music.

ANNIE ATE JAM

Traditional Rhyme
Arranged by Jim Solomon

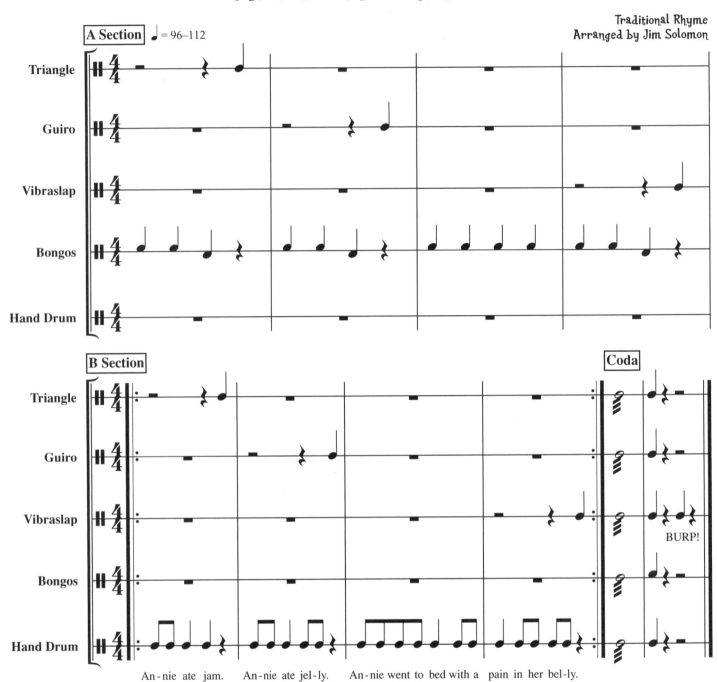

An-nie ate jam. An-nie ate jel-ly. An-nie went to bed with a pain in her bel-ly.

FORM:

- **Introduction**
  (speak rhyme)
- **A**
- **B**
- **Coda**

TEACHING SUGGESTIONS:

1. Tell students: "Find the pattern of the numbers." Teacher then speaks the numbers of the bongo part (1 2 3 – 1 2 3 – 1 2 3 4 1 2 3) while performing triangle, guiro and vibraslap parts.
2. Repeat step one with the class counting along.
3. Say: "We need drummers!" Teacher demonstrates hand drum part from **B** section.
4. Say: "There are some 'painful' words that go with this. Find out why." Teacher speaks rhyme, students answer.
5. Echo speak words from chart.
6. Clap the rhythm of the rhyme.
7. All perform the rhythm on hand drums.
8. Review bongo part numbers, then have tryouts.
9. Teach the **Coda**.
10. Review and perform.

Have students listen for the contrast in timbre: metal, wood, drums and special effects (vibraslap).

SEE A PIN

Traditional
Arranged by Jim Solomon

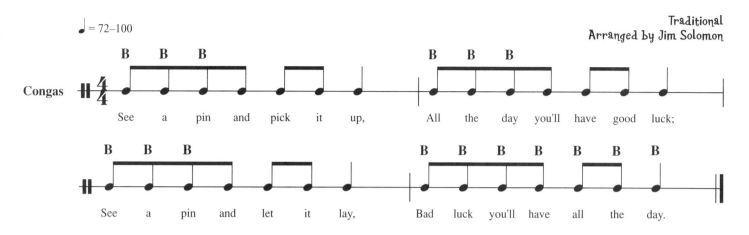

♩ = 72–100

Congas

| B | B | B |
See a pin and pick it up,
| B | B | B |
All the day you'll have good luck;

| B | B | B |
See a pin and let it lay,
| B | B | B | B | B | B | B |
Bad luck you'll have all the day.

*Congas: All notes marked with **B** are Basses; all others are Tones*

ACCOMPANYING PARTS

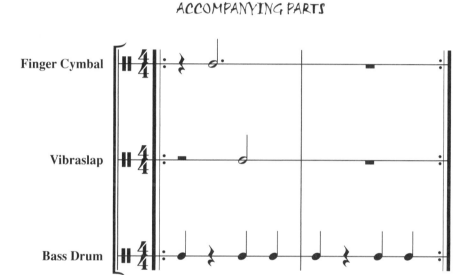

Finger Cymbal

Vibraslap

Bass Drum

FORM:

- **A**: congas with accompaniment one time
- **B**: soloist: either improvise or play rhythm of words; bass drum continues
- continue **A B A B A**

- Recommend playing one thick finger cymbal with a triangle beater for a beautiful sound.
- Finger cymbal occurs each time on the word "pin."
- Vibraslap occurs on "pick" and "let."

TEACHING SUGGESTIONS:

1. Have the students define "pen" and "pin."
   Say: "Which one (pen or pin) do you think is in this rhyme?" Teacher speaks rhyme. "Pin."
2. Say: "Is the pattern of Basses the same?" Teacher plays rhyme on conga. "No."
3. Show chart of words with Basses marked with "B." Say: "Watch where I clap." Teacher speaks rhyme, claps on Basses.
4. Students speak rhyme and clap on Basses.
5. Play on congas, then add other parts.
6. Set up instruments in a circle, alternating types—use as many finger cymbals (and triangles) as you have. Play rhyme once, then have a soloist, then rotate to the next instrument in the circle (Rotating Circle).

This arrangement has a thin texture. It will still require focus from your third graders to play the finger cymbal and vibraslap accurately.

CHARLIE, CHARLIE, IN THE TUB

Traditional Rhyme
Arranged by Jim Solomon

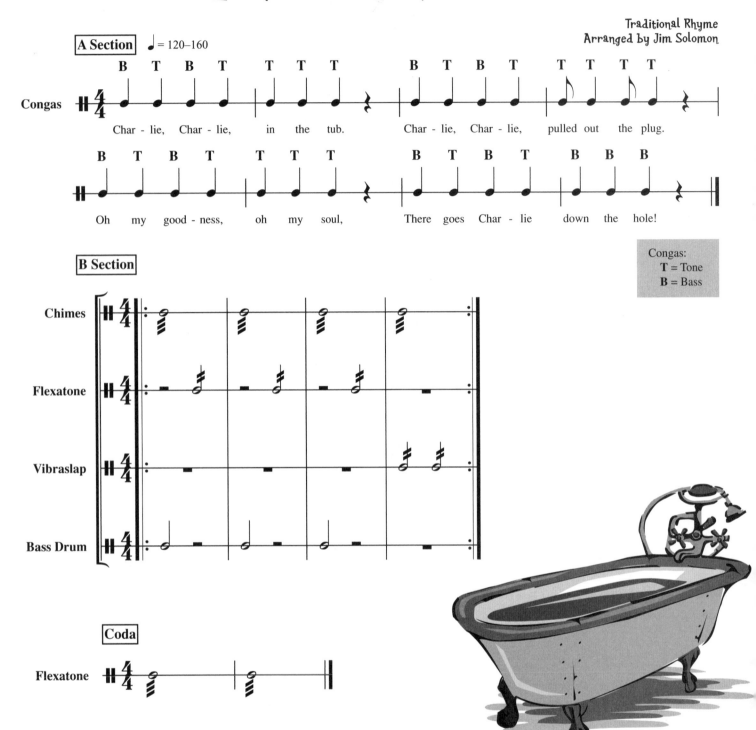

Congas:
T = Tone
B = Bass

FORM:

- **A**: words spoken
- **A1**: congas play rhythm
- **B**
- **C**: **A1** + **B** together
- **Coda**

TEACHING SUGGESTIONS:

1. Say: "What happened to Charlie? Is this real or a joke?" Teacher speaks rhyme, students answer.
2. Say: "Let's see if the clapping pattern changes." Teacher speaks rhyme again, claps on Basses. "Yes."
3. "Clap with me." Teacher speaks rhyme again.
4. Show chart and have students read words and clap on Basses.
5. Pat rhythm.
6. Add other parts, review and perform.

Have students listen for and interpret the effect of the special effects instruments. (The chimes mimic the sound of water going down the hole.)

ICE CREAM

Traditional
Arranged by Jim Solomon

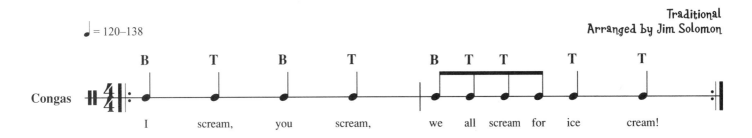

Congas:	Cowbell:
T = Tone	**M** = Mouth
B = Bass	**H** = Heel

ACCOMPANYING PARTS

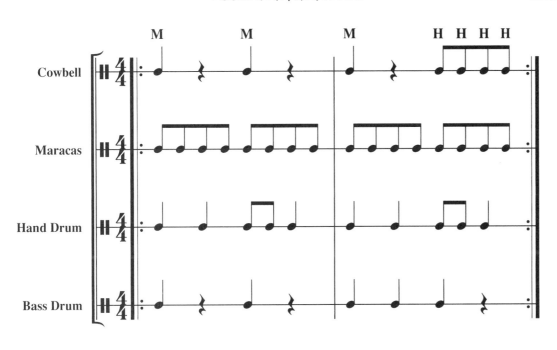

FORM:

- Devise your own form using a few or all of the following ideas.
- Layer in
- Have improvisational sections
- Have a soloist play the main rhythm
- Have group solos on their parts
- Other

TEACHING SUGGESTIONS:

1. Say: "What are pronouns?" Students answer, then teacher speaks rhyme.
2. Students identify "I, you, we."
3. "Watch when I clap." Teacher speaks again, claps on pronouns. "When did I clap?"
4. "Join me clapping on each pronoun." Teacher speaks and all clap on pronouns.
5. Students say rhyme and clap on pronouns.
6. Echo pat rhythm of words.
7. Echo pat rhythm of words playing pronouns on knees (Basses), and other words on upper thighs (Tones).
8. Add other parts with simultaneous imitation.

Leave out Cowbell and/or Hand Drum if there are too many parts for a class. The main rhythm is appropriate for second grade if those parts are left out.

PAIRS OR PEARS

Traditional
Arranged by Jim Solomon

FORM:

- **A**
- **B**
- **B**

Congas:
T = Tone
B = Bass

TEACHING SUGGESTIONS:

1. Students define "pair" and "pear."
2. "How many were left in the tree?" Teacher speaks rhyme. Students explain.
3. The rhythm of the rhyme's first eight beats is very easy; the last eight beats are a little tricky, so focus on the last eight beats first when you echo speak, then echo pat the rhythms. Use a chart of the rhyme and instrument parts.
4. Students create words to fit temple block rhythm, then add special effects instruments. Have students rotate around to different parts (Rotating Circle).

Have students listen for the contrast in timbre: metal, wood, drums and special effects.

MISTER EAST GAVE A FEAST

Traditional
Arranged by Jim Solomon

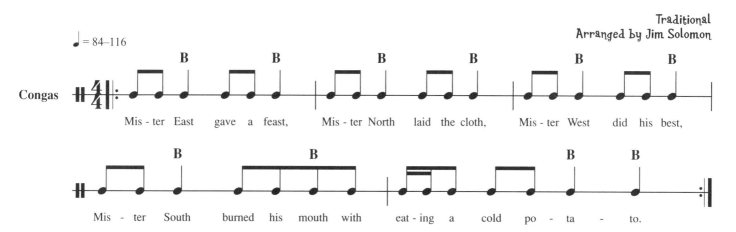

Mis - ter East gave a feast, Mis - ter North laid the cloth, Mis - ter West did his best,

Mis - ter South burned his mouth with eat - ing a cold po - ta - to.

Congas: All strokes are Tones except for the ones marked as Basses (B).

ACCOMPANYING PARTS

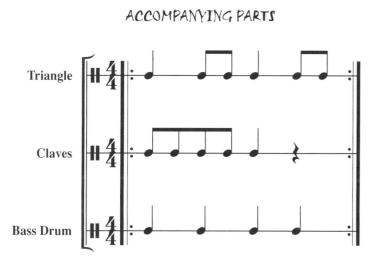

FORM:

- **A**
- **B**: (soloist plays rhyme or improvises)
- **A**
- Continue alternating soloists and the **A** section as students move to different instruments in the alternating circle.

TEACHING SUGGESTIONS:

1. Say: "Could this really happen?" Teacher speaks rhyme. "No."
2. Say: "Is the pattern of Basses the same throughout?" Teacher plays rhythm on conga. "No."
3. Teach this rhythm backwards (from the end first). Echo speak measure 5, then 4 and 5, then have them read the entire rhyme. Then echo pat measure 5, then 4 and 5, then have them pat entire rhyme.
4. All students practice drum part.
5. Students create food words (for the "feast") that match the triangle, claves and bass drum parts.
6. Set up circle of alternating instruments (Rotating Circle), i.e., drum, triangle, drum claves, etc. Students rotate around circle and play appropriate parts.

> This is a five measure rhyme, so it is slightly unpredictable—students must always think the words to play the changes at the end accurately.

ONCE A YEAR

Traditional
Arranged by Jim Solomon

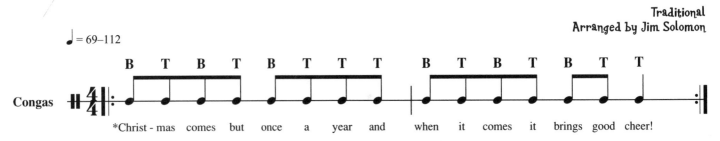

Word substitution: for "Christmas" insert "Summer," "Kwanzaa," "Birthday," "Hanukkah" (adjust the rhythm accordingly).

ACCOMPANYING PARTS

FORM:

Students create their own form using the following ideas:
- Introduction
- Interludes
- Decide how many times to play the main rhyme
- Improvisation

Congas:
T = Tone
B = Bass

TEACHING SUGGESTIONS:

1. Isolate the location of the Basses. Play those first with the "pencil hand."

At a quick tempo, my third graders struggled with this. At a slow tempo, they did well. This piece can be used with fifth graders by having them create new drum parts and playing at a quicker tempo.

NELLIE BLIGH

Traditional
Arranged by Jim Solomon

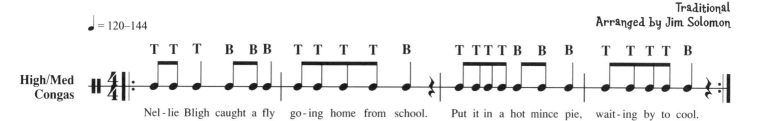

♩ = 120–144

High/Med Congas

T T T B B B T T T T B   T T T T B B B   T T T T B

Nel-lie Bligh caught a fly go-ing home from school. Put it in a hot mince pie, wait-ing by to cool.

ACCOMPANYING PARTS

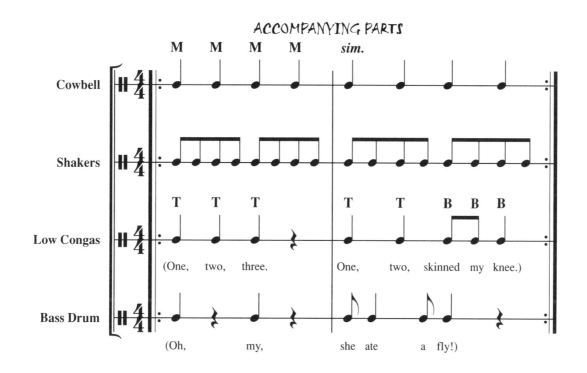

Cowbell — M M M M *sim.*

Shakers

Low Congas — T T T   T T B B B

(One, two, three. One, two, skinned my knee.)

Bass Drum

(Oh, my, she ate a fly!)

FORM:

- Create your own.
- Use instrumental interludes or improvisation in alternating sections.

Congas:	Cowbell:
T = Tone	**M** = Mouth
B = Bass	

TEACHING SUGGESTIONS:

1. Say: "Does the pattern of Basses stay the same?" Teacher plays rhyme on conga. "Yes."
2. "What's strange about this rhyme?" Teacher speaks, students answer. Say: "I'm glad Nellie's not cooking my food."
3. Echo speak, then read from chart.
4. Students read and clap on Basses.
5. Practice rhythm with patschen (patting thighs), then play on drum.
6. Read and learn other parts.

BIG TURTLE SAT

Traditional Rhyme
Arranged by Jim Solomon

FORM:

- **A**
- **Interlude**
- **B**
- **A1**: (guiro/woodblock continue)
- **B**

Con a:
  T = one

TEACHING SUGGESTIONS:

. Use or s "Bi tur-t e sat" to tea h rhythm o first three measures
  o **A** se tion.
. Use rhyme to tea h main rhythm o **B** se tion.
.   n e uiro/ oo b o k enter in the **Interlude**, they ne er stop
  unti the en .
. Stu ents an reate impro isationa se tion s by ha in
  instruments impro ise o er bass   rum/ uiro/ oo b o k parts.
5.   his pie e an be use   or tea hin   rea in o syn opation.

Ha e stu ents isten or the ontrast in timbre: meta ,   oo an   rum.

SLEEPER'S SONG

Class Composition
Arranged by Jim Solomon

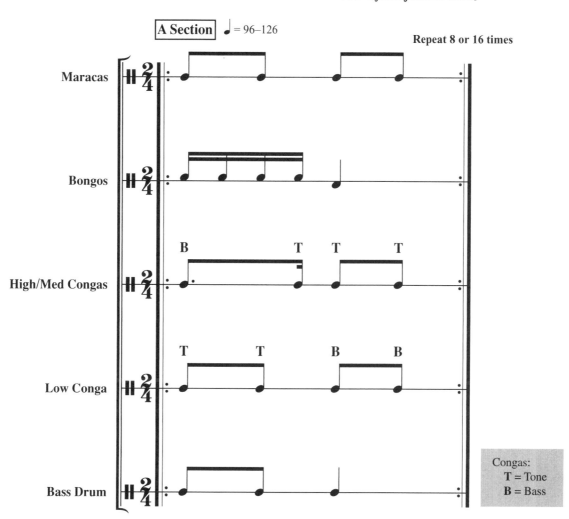

The parts for this piece were developed by a fourth grade class after being given the main rhythm, i.e., the high/medium conga part. The entire piece consists of two beat ostinato patterns! The location of the accents (Basses) gives it dynamic tension.

FORM:

- **A**: repeat above rhythms 8 or 16 times.
- **B, C,** and further sections: one part at a time continue ("Group Solos") OR individuals improvise over bass drum and maracas.
- Continue alternating group solos or individual improvisations with the **A** section.

TEACHING SUGGESTIONS:

1. Learn parts by echo play. Create words for parts that give any difficulty.

RAIN, RAIN CANON

Traditional
Arranged by Jim Solomon

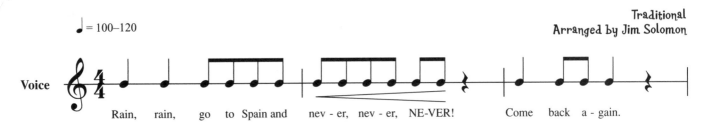

Rain, rain, go to Spain and nev-er, nev-er, NE-VER! Come back a-gain.

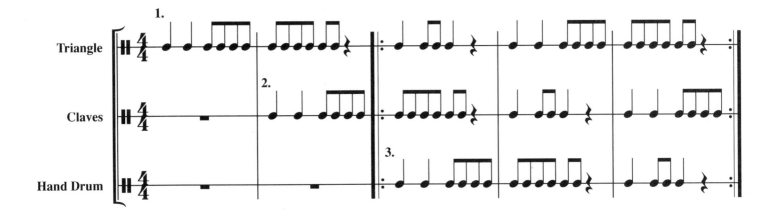

FORM:

- Voice unison, one time
- Instruments unison, one time
- Instruments in 3-part canon playing the rhythm of the words, multiple times!

TEACHING SUGGESTIONS:

1. Ask the class, "Do we really want this to happen?" Teacher speaks rhyme. "No!" Say: "Why not? We NEED rain!"
2. Echo speak rhyme with precision, with a crescendo in the second measure.
3. Clap rhythm unison. Stress precision and accuracy in the clapping.
4. Play the rhythm unison on triangles, claves and hand drums—rotate around a circle of instruments set in the pattern of triangle/claves/hand drum so all have multiple turns on each instrument. Substitute instruments for those you don't have enough of (for example, sticks for claves).
5. NEXT CLASS—speak unison, then speak canon 2 parts, then canon 3 parts.
6. Play unison, then 3-part canon on instruments. (If they are ready, perform in canon in the first class.)

Have students listen for the timbre contrast in the parts: metal, wood and drum.

JACK & JILL

Traditional
Arranged by Jim Solomon

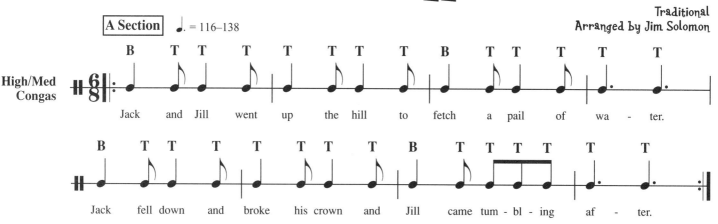

Jack and Jill went up the hill to fetch a pail of wa - ter.

Jack fell down and broke his crown and Jill came tum - bl - ing af - ter.

ACCOMPANYING PARTS

Congas:	Cowbell:
T = Tone	**M** = Mouth
B = Bass	**H** = Heel

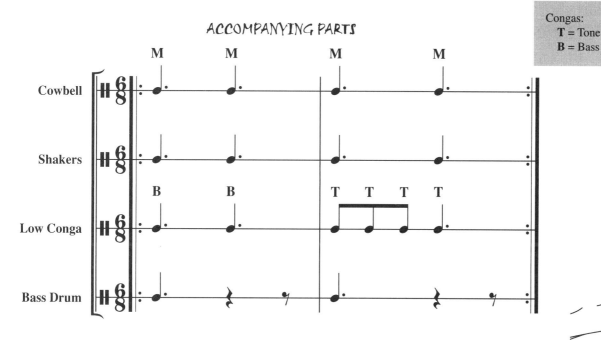

VERSION 2: To markedly increase the difficulty level, add the following cowbell and high conga parts.

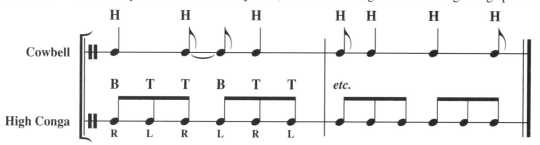

FORM:

Rondo:
- **A**
- **B***
- **A**
- **C***
- **A**

***B** and **C** sections: Conga improvisation—utilize the talents of your group, i.e., do Question & Answer with many taking a turn, or have one student improvise for each section.

TEACHING SUGGESTIONS:

1. Say: "Does the pattern of the Basses change? " Teacher plays rhyme on conga. "No."
2. "Clap on each Bass with me." Teacher plays again, students clap.
3. "This comes from an old rhyme you probably knew before you ever went to school. Dig into your memory bank to figure out what it is!" Play again if necessary. Students identify rhyme.
4. Pat rhythm on legs.
5. Pat rhythm on thigh and play knee for the Basses.
6. Play on drums.
7. Students create words for challenging parts.

PETER WHITE

Traditional
Arranged by Jim Solomon

FORM:

- **A**: All instruments
- **B**: One instrument (temple blocks or sound effects) improvises over bass drum
- **A**
- Continue alternating improvisers with the **A** section.

TEACHING SUGGESTIONS:

1. Make a chart of words with special effects words marked.
2. Say: "Should you make fun of people for the way they look? That's not big-hearted. Listen to this rhyme. Find out why Peter walked the wrong way." Teacher speaks, students answer.
3. Echo speak words precisely from chart.
4. Practice rhythm, add sound effects and bass drum, and perform.

Have students listen for the contrast in timbre: wood, metal, drum and special effects.

ONCE I CAUGHT A FISH ALIVE

Traditional Rhyme
Arranged by Jim Solomon

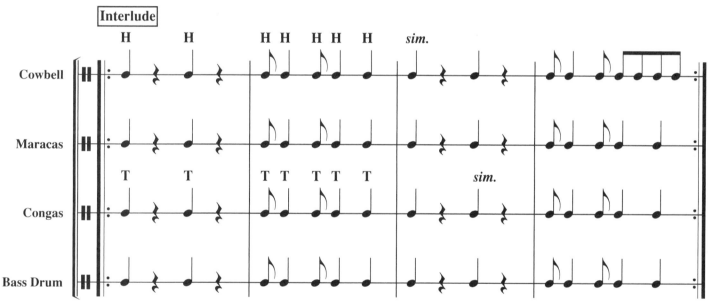

FORM:

- **A**
- **Interlude**
- **A**
- **Interlude** with improvisation
- **A**

Congas:	Cowbell:
T = Tone	**M** = Mouth
B = Bass	**H** = Heel

TEACHING SUGGESTIONS:

1. Say: "Time to go fishing! Find out if the pattern of Basses stays the same or if it changes dramatically." Teacher plays **A** section conga part. "Changes."
2. Say: "Clap with me on Basses." Teacher plays again.
3. Ask: "What happened to the fish?" Teacher speaks rhyme.
4. Echo speak and learn. Do last half of rhyme first, paying close attention to the word "and."
5. Play rhythm with body percussion, then on drums.
6. Learn bass drum part by writing the numbers 1 2 3 4 1 2 3 4 and circling the numbers where the bass drum plays.
7. Add the other parts and perform.
8. It will take fourth graders several days of practice to get the main rhythm.

See the Elephant Jump the Fence

Traditional
Arranged by Jim Solomon

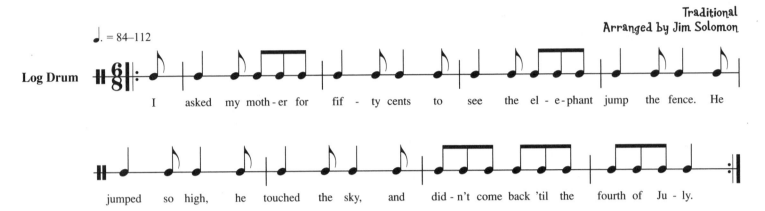

I asked my moth-er for fif-ty cents to see the el-e-phant jump the fence. He

jumped so high, he touched the sky, and did-n't come back 'til the fourth of Ju-ly.

ACCOMPANYING PARTS

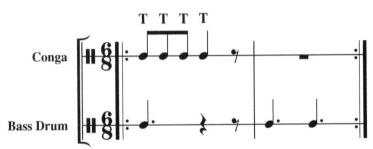

SPECIAL EFFECTS ACCOMPANIMENT:

- Tambourine   play on "fif-ty cents"
- Flexitone   play on "jump the fence"
- Triangle   play on "touched the sky"
- Snare Drum   play on "fourth of Ju-ly"

FORM:

- **A**: Speak with special effects instruments
- **Interlude**: Conga and Bass Drum
- **A1**: Log drum plays rhythm with all accompaniment

Have students create a more extended Form.

Conga:
T = Tone

TEACHING SUGGESTIONS:

1. Present this as a study in timbre: wood plays the main rhythm, membranes play main accompaniment parts, then metal and membrane play special effects.
2. Say: "Where do you hear the straight eighth notes?" Perform log drum part. "At the end."
3. "This rhythm comes from an old rhyme that is slightly crazy." Teach the rhyme, practice the main rhythm.
4. Teach conga and bass drum parts. Add sound effects and Form.
5. For further study, ask students to revise the Form and experiment with different entrances, etc.

Have students listen for and interpret the effect of the special effects instruments.

CHRISTMAS IS COMING

Traditional Rhyme
Arranged by Jim Solomon

Christ-mas is com-ing, the geese are get-ting fat. Please do put a pen-ny in the old man's hat. If you have-n't got a pen-ny, a half pen-ny will do; If you have-n't got a half pen-ny then God bless you!

Congas play entire rhythm with Tones until the three Basses in the last measure.

Conga:
T = Tone

ACCOMPANYING PARTS

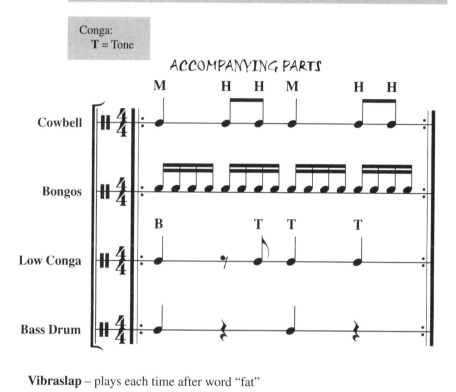

Cowbell

Bongos

Low Conga

Bass Drum

Vibraslap – plays each time after word "fat"

FORM:

- **A**: speak rhyme (with vitality!)
- **A1**: congas/bass drum play
- **A2**: speak with congas/bass drum
- **A3**: congas/bass drum play with bongos/low conga/cowbell joining
- **A4**: speak with all instruments playing

TEACHING SUGGESTIONS:

1. Say: "How many times do I clap my hands?" Teacher speaks rhyme and claps once after the word "fat." (vibraslap part)
2. Say: "Clap with me after 'fat,' then watch where I clap three more times." Teacher speaks, claps after "fat" and on the words, "God bless you." (location of three Basses).
3. "Clap with me all four times." Teacher speaks rhyme again, students clap with teacher.
4. Show a chart of the rhyme. Echo speak each line very precisely with vitality until students have it, then speak the whole.
5. Add instruments.

The conga part is challenging at a quick tempo, but your best players will be able play it. This piece can give variety to December Chorus performances.

THUMP THUMP

Jim Solomon

Bass Drum

Voice

Lis-ten to my heart beat thump, thump. Lis-ten to my heart beat thump, thump.

Lis-ten to my heart, Lis-ten to my heart, Lis-ten to my heart beat, heart beat, heart beat, heart beat!

High/Med Congas

Cowbell

Vibraslap

Low Congas

(Thump, thump, lis-ten to my heart beat. Thump, thump, lis-ten to my heart beat.

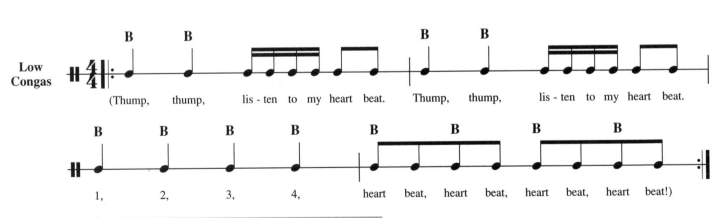

1, 2, 3, 4, heart beat, heart beat, heart beat, heart beat!)

*Congas: All notes marked with **B** are Basses; all others are Tones*

NOTES

1. Chorus (speakers) alternate 16 beats of "chest thump" with 16 beats of "low clap" throughout the piece, even when they are not speaking.
2. This can be performed by a Drum Group without a Chorus with exactly the same Form, except eliminate the chest thumps and claps by the performers when they start playing an instrument.

> "Chest thump"– lightly thump beat (same as bass drum part) on chest with L hand
> "Low clap"– clap beat (same as bass drum part), palm to palm, with cupped hands

FORM:

Additive

1. **Introduction**: 8 beats Bass Drum
2. Intensely whisper rhyme with chest thump
3. Powerfully speak rhyme with low clap
4. High drummers play rhythm of the words; Chorus chest thumps
5. High/medium drummers play rhythm of the words; Chorus low claps
6. Cowbell adds in with previous players; Chorus chest thumps
7. Vibraslap adds in with previous players; Chorus low claps
8. Low congas add in with previous players; Chorus chest thumps
9. Repeat #8; Chorus low claps
10. Chorus adds in powerful voices with chest thump
11. Repeat #10 with low claps
12. **Coda**: Drumroll 4 beats, stop on 5th beat

TEACHING SUGGESTIONS

1. Say: "Count how many Basses are in the main rhythm." Teacher performs on conga. "Eight."
2. Say: "Find the words where the Basses happen." Teacher plays and speaks, students identify.
3. Say: "Clap on the Bass words with me." Teacher plays and speaks again.
4. Echo speak and learn words from a chart.
5. Students whisper, then speak entire piece, with the body percussion in parts 2 and 3 of the form.
6. Practice and add instrument parts. Learn the form and perform.

> I teach any difficult instrument parts to my instrumental group at a separate time from the chorus rehearsal.

THE BOB

Camp Rhythm
Arranged by Jim Solomon

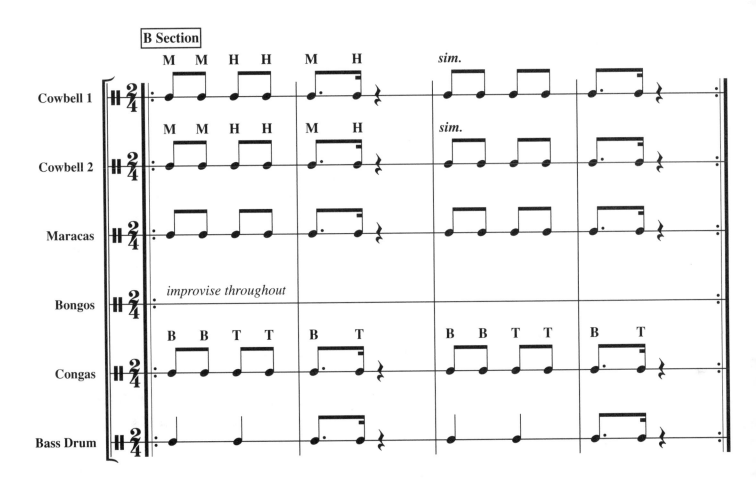

FORM:

- **A**
- **B**
- **A**
- **B**
- **A**
- and so on

Congas:
   T = Tone
   B = Bass

Cowbell:
   M = Mouth
   H = Heel

TEACHING SUGGESTIONS:

1. Ask question, "How many Basses at the end of the main rhythm?" Teacher plays. "Four."
2. "Play those four Basses on your knee when I play them." Students play those with teacher at the end of the pattern.
3. "Play all the Basses with me."
4. "Play the whole rhythm with me."
5. Students create words for it.
6. Teach **B** section, "The Conga," with words, "Now let's play the con-ga."
7. Students create movement for **A** section: Teacher plays main rhythm on conga throughout. "Move one arm with the music…move the other arm… move both arms…add your shoulders…add some other parts of your body with that [hips, knees, etc.]…Now you are doing 'The Bob,' your own made up moves."
8. Dance a conga line for **B** section rhythm:
      | step, step, step, side | step, step, step, other side |
9. Add cowbell, maracas, bass drum.
10. Pick a player to improvise during **B** section.

This piece works well if you have one instrument for every two students. Pair up the students—one person plays while the other person dances their own improvised dance behind the player. Students who are uncomfortable dancing can tilt their shoulders and sway from side to side with a "side-touch, side touch" step. When all instruments are cued to stop playing the **A** section, the instrument players stand up in front of their instruments, then dance in a conga line around behind the instruments while those who were dancing take over the instruments and play the **B** section ("The Conga"). Cue those players back to the **A** section rhythm when it feels right! The students who were just playing the instruments are now the dancers standing behind their partners who are now the players.

To make the change from **A** section to **B** section and back again, the students must know each section very well independently of the other. Practice by saying, "Play the Conga…Play it again…Play the Bob…" etc.

This piece is called "The Bob" after a student whose 'dance moves' were admired.

FROM WIBBLETON TO WOBBLETON

Anonymous
Arranged by Jim Solomon

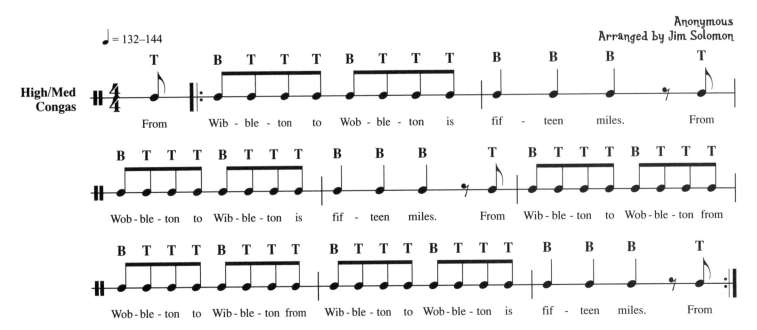

ACCOMPANYING PARTS

FORM:

- Devise your own form using a few or all of the following ideas.
- Layer in
- Have improvisational sections
- Have a soloist play the main rhythm
- Have group solos on their parts

Congas:	Cowbell:
T = Tone	**M** = Mouth
B = Bass	**H** = Heel

TEACHING SUGGESTIONS:

1. Ask question: "Is the pattern of Basses the same throughout or does it change?" Teacher plays rhyme on conga. "The pattern changes."
2. "Clap every time three Basses are played in a row." Teacher plays rhyme again, students clap.
3. "What are the words where the three Basses are played?" Teacher speaks rhyme, students identify "fif-teen miles."
4. "Who can say these words precisely?" Echo speak rhyme.
5. Students speak whole rhyme, clap on Basses.
6. Patsch rhythm of whole rhyme in slow motion.
7. Patsch rhythm at a moderate tempo, then play on drums.
8. Learn other parts with simultaneous imitation. Create words for any parts that give difficulty.

A Sieve

Traditional
Arranged by Jim Solomon

FORM:

An "Additive Rondo"
- **A**
- **B**
- **A + B**
- **C**
- **A + B + C**
- **D**
- **A + B + C + D**
- **E**
- **A + B + C + D + E**
- FINALE: All instruments play
  A section rhythm unison

TEACHING SUGGESTIONS:

1. This is an excellent piece for students ready to read $\frac{6}{8}$ meter, as many basic $\frac{6}{8}$ patterns are used. First teach each part by ear. As the teacher plays each pattern, students brainstorm words to fit.
2. Show the notation and the counting.
3. Have students listen for the contrast in timbre.

> This piece requires focus, mental intensity, and precision.

POLY 2 WITH 3*

Jim Solomon

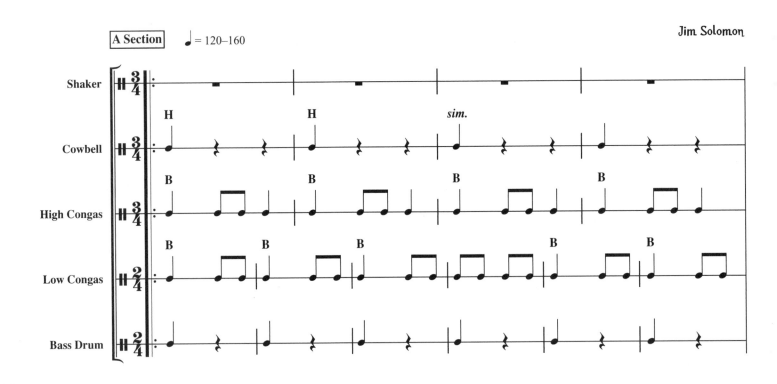

*Congas: All notes marked with **B** are Basses; all others are Tones*

Polymeter – two contrasting meters played concurrently

B Section

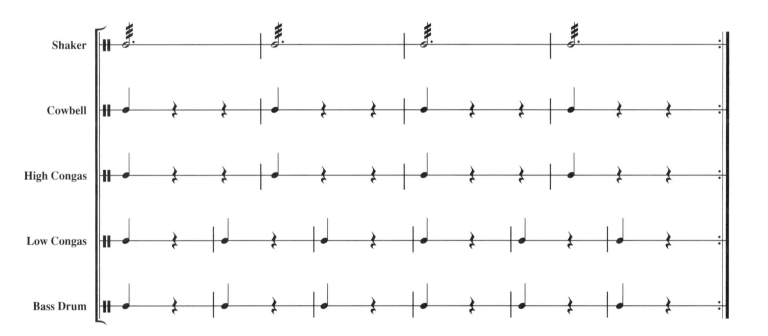

FORM:
- **A**
- **B**
- **A**
- **B**
- **A**
- **Coda** (drumroll!)

TEACHING SUGGESTIONS:
1. Students create words to match the rhythms of the high and low conga parts in **A** section.
2. Count the **B** section, play on first beat of each measure.

The critical consideration is that all players maintain precise tempo.

eastside, westside

Jim Solomon

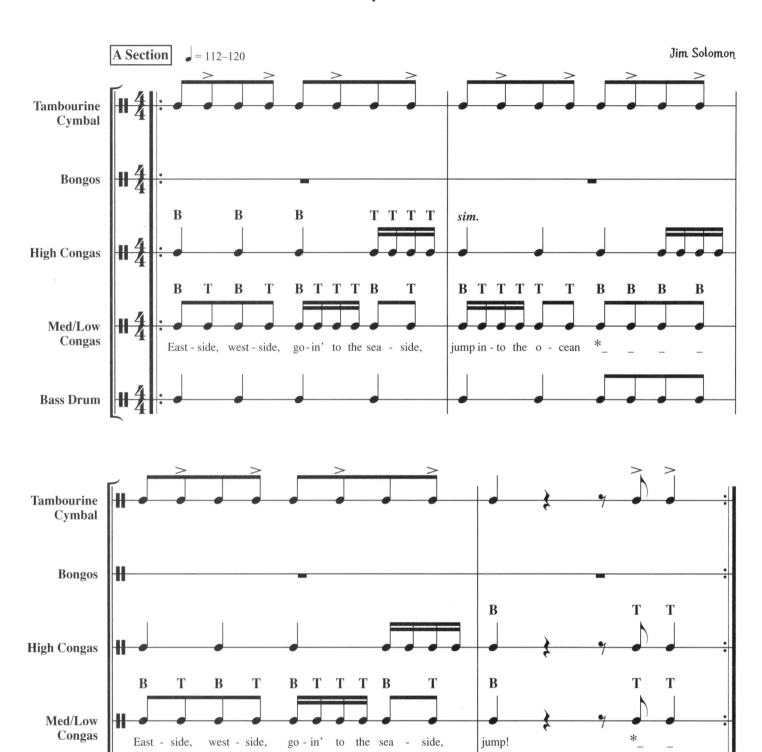

Players decide on words to fill in at the end of measures 2 and 4.

Interlude #1: High conga and tambourine/cymbal parts continue for four measures.

Interlude #2: Bass drum part continues for four measures; group can create words to call out during this part.

A1 Section

FORM:

- **A**
- **Interlude #1**
- **A**
- **Interlude #2**
- **A1** (A + bongos)

TEACHING SUGGESTIONS:

1. Say: "Watch where I clap. Does the pattern change?" Teacher speaks rhyme and claps on medium/low conga part Basses. "Yes."
2. Ask: "How many times do I clap without speaking a word?" Teacher speaks and claps Basses again. "Four."
3. Say: "Clap with me."
4. Show chart of rhyme. Say: "Read and clap with me."
5. Students create words for four claps after "ocean." (Funny is good here!)
6. Perform main rhythm with body percussion. Practice several times in slow motion before picking up the tempo.
7. Add other parts and perform.

ALLIGATOR BONGO, ALLIGATOR DRUM

Camp Piece
Arranged by Jim Solomon

♩ = 120–138

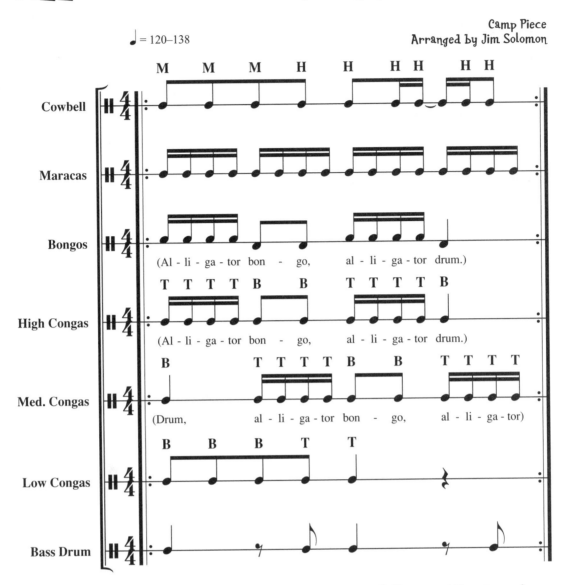

The parts for this piece were developed by a summer camp Orff group. All parts are four beat ostinato patterns. The entrance of the medium conga in canon drives this piece.

FORM:

- Layer instruments in:
  1. low conga
  2. bass drum/maracas/cowbell
  3. bongos/high conga
- Let it "cook"*
- Utilize "solo group" sections and/or improvisational sections depending on the abilities of your group.
- Begin medium conga. Its part creates a one beat canon.

Congas:	Cowbell:
T = Tone	**M** = Mouth
B = Bass	**H** = Heel

TEACHING SUGGESTIONS:

1. Speak words at tempo.
2. Speak words in canon—have second entrance begin with "Drum."
3. Perform words unison with patschen body percussion.
4. Perform words in canon with patschen body percussion.
5. Add other parts—*work for precision of parts in unison before performing canon.*

Medium congas can play the bongo/high conga part until switching to canon. Have low conga players develop sound, movement and gestures to dramatize the rest on the 4th beat of their part.

*Cook is a slang word used in jazz, meaning performing or proceeding well.

CONFUSION

Jim Solomon

FORM:

- **A**
- **B**
- **A**
- **B**
- **A1** (select an instrument from the **B** section to improvise in the last **A** section)

TEACHING SUGGESTIONS:

1. All of the **A** section is based on the pattern ♫ ♫ ♩ —each instrument begins the pattern on a different beat, creating a 4-part canon.
    - tambourine begins the pattern on beat 1
    - claves begin the pattern on beat 2
    - bass drum begins the pattern on beat 3
    - cowbell begins the pattern on beat 4

2. Have all students play the main pattern ♫ ♫ ♩ and create words for it. Pay close attention to the accents when creating the words. Then have each instrument say "Wait" on each beat until it's time for its entrance, i.e., the claves player whose pattern begins on the second beat will say: "Wait ♫ ♫ ♩"

3. After the students have had sufficient experience with this, try them all starting at beat 1 together. (This will take practice!)

4. Regarding the "wild, chaotic, a-rhythmic" improvisation, suggest that all players don't play all the time. Tell them to pick their spots and play unpredictably.

> Have students listen for the timbre contrast in the **A** section and the special effects in the **B** section.

TOTALLY CHICKENISH

Class Composition
Arranged by Jim Solomon

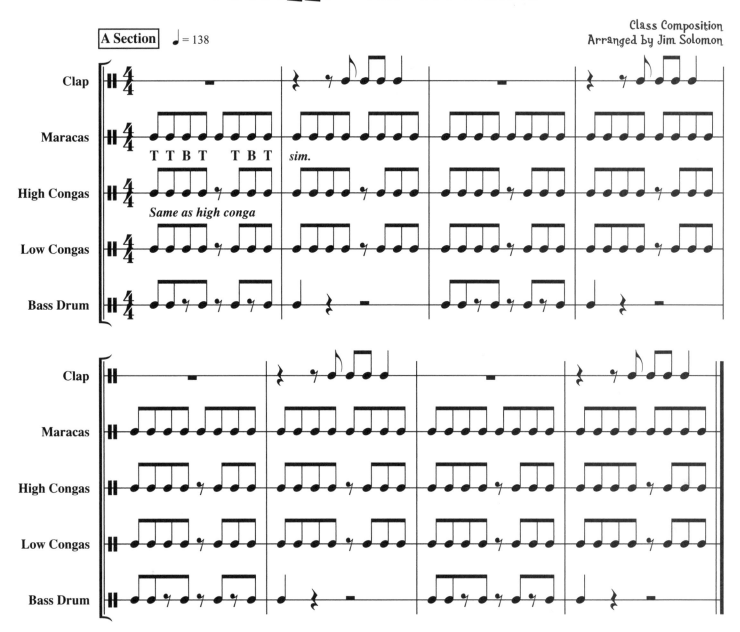

Interlude: Bass drummer improvises. All point to the drummer and chant, "Go ___(name of drummer)___!"

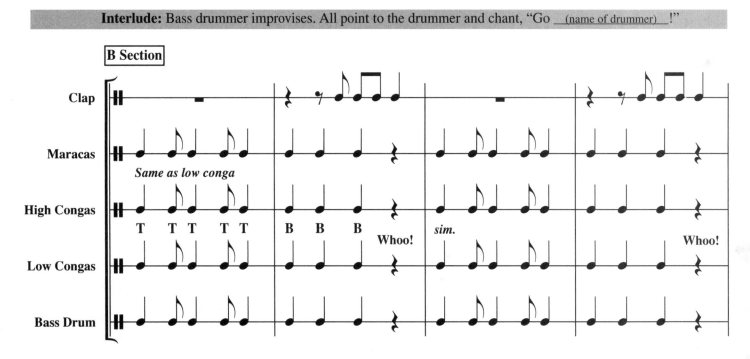

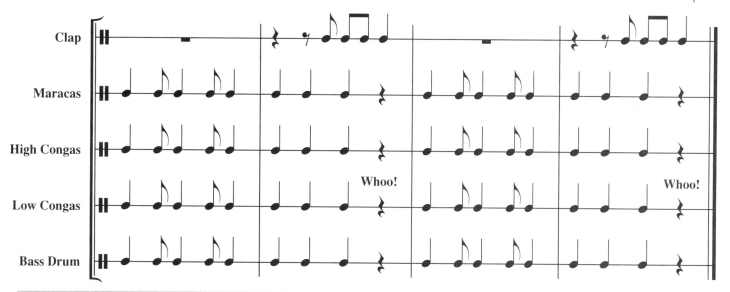

Interlude: repeat bass drum improvisation

C Section

FORM:

- **A**
- **Interlude**
- **B**
- **Interlude**
- **C**

Congas: **T** = Tone   **B** = Bass

TEACHING SUGGESTIONS:

1. Students create words for **A** section high conga part and bass drum part, also for **B** section main rhythm.
2. Practice those rhythms thoroughly—they are combined in the **C** section.
3. Need a very secure improviser on the bass drum part.

"Chicken Dancers" dance the traditional dance and do the hand claps: pinch hands 4 times (4 eighth notes timing), flap "wings" (elbows) 4 times, twist down to floor, do hand claps.

JUNGLE

Jim Solomon

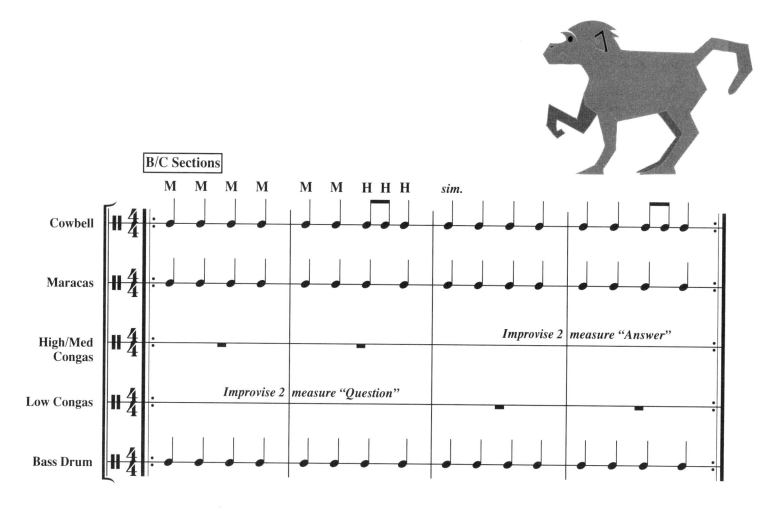

FORM:

Rondo:
- A
- B
- A
- C
- A

Congas:	Cowbell:
B = Bass,	**M** = Mouth
all others	**H** = Heel
are Tones	

TEACHING SUGGESTIONS:

1. Make a chart with all parts written out.
2. Vocalize each part with jungle words that the class creates or with cool nonsense syllables.
3. Clap with the Basses of the main rhythm (High/Med conga part).
4. Play it with body percussion, then on drums.
5. The **A** section low conga and maraca parts can be added quickly.
6. Students may need to hear the cowbell and bass drum parts repeatedly over several days, then have tryouts for those two parts. Challenge them! For instance, say: "The cowbell is an adult part. I wonder if anyone can play it?"

The contrast between the highly syncopated **A** section and the straight, on-the-beat **B/C** sections will provide excitement. The **B/C** section accompaniment also provides a very secure background for the improvisers.

LOST AT "C" RONDO

Jim Solomon

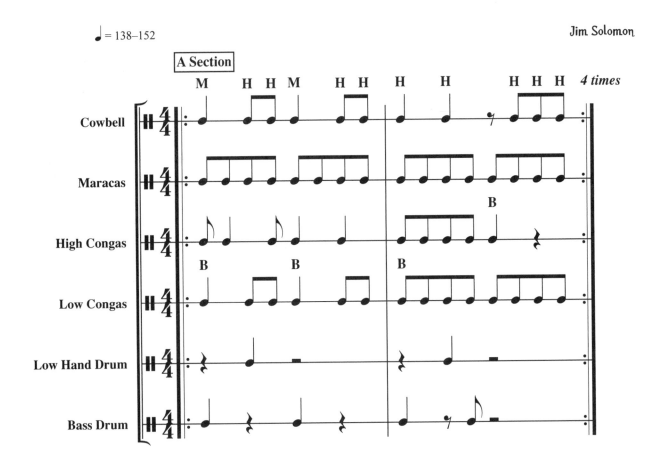

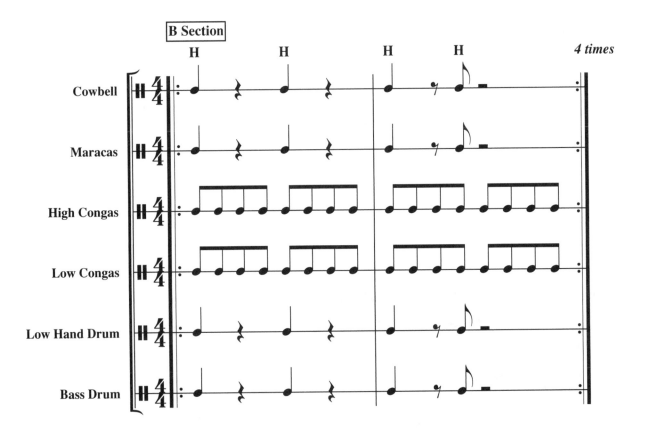

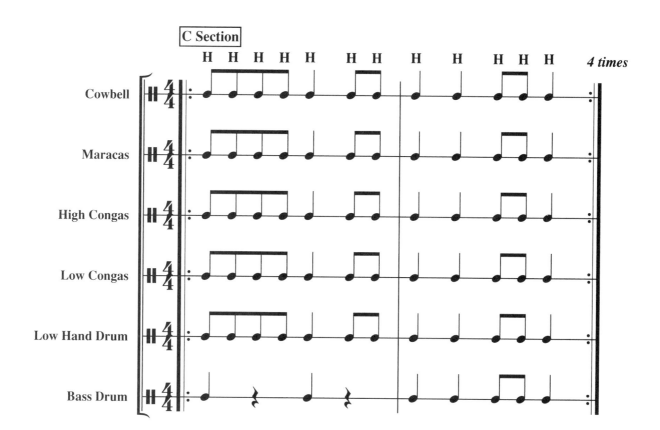

FORM:

- A
- B
- A
- C
- A
- C

TEACHING SUGGESTIONS:

1. Learn one section at a time. Let each section become set in the players' memory before starting the next.
2. Explain normal construction of a Rondo (**ABACA**). However, this Rondo goes back to the **C** and "gets lost" (stops) there.
3. Show a visual of the **A** section. Play high conga pattern. Develop words for it. Funny is good! Do this for all challenging parts.

Congas:
B = Bass,
all others
are Tones

Cowbell:
M = Mouth
H = Heel

ASHES TO ASHES

Traditional Rhyme
Arranged by Jim Solomon

B/C Sections: individual drummer(s) improvise for the length of the rhyme four times over cowbell/shaker/bass drum parts. This can be done by one, two, or four drummers.

FORM:

- **Introduction**: layer in instruments
- **A**
- **B**: improvisation
- **A**
- **C**: improvisation
- **A**

TEACHING SUGGESTIONS:

1. Straight eighth notes in $\frac{6}{8}$ require shifting of the accents from R to L hands. Start practice on the high conga part first while counting **1** 2 3 **4** 5 6. This part is very difficult for elementary/ middle school players and will take time to develop.
2. Teach main rhythm with rhyme.
3. Teach cowbell and bass drum parts by modeling them frequently and "getting them into the players' ears." Have players develop words for them.

Congas:	Bass Drum:	Cowbell:
T = Tone	**T** = Tone	Play all
B = Bass	**M** = Mute	on Heel

BUTTERFLY

Jim Solomon

FORM:

Additive

- **A**: recorder and guitar (simple "thumb-pluck" accompaniment)
- **A** + conga/bass drum (guitar strums full chords vigorously!)
- **A** + conga/bass drum + recorder descant
- Interlude: conga/bass drum
- **A** + conga/bass drum + recorder descant

Conga:
- **T** = Tone
- **B** = Bass

TEACHING SUGGESTIONS:

1. As the rhythm is tricky, students should hear it numerous times before playing the whole song.
2. Ask: "How many times do you hear 'G G GA G G GG'?" Teacher plays song. (one time, last two measures)
3. Students sing that part.
4. Students play that part while you sing entirely.
5. Add D, G, D, G from first half of song.
6. Continue to build in this way.
7. Add descant part from notation.

BRISA CAMBIANDO*

Jim Solomon

*Brisa Cambiando = Changing Breeze

FORM:

- **A**
- **Interlude**
- **A**
- **Interlude**
- **A**

TEACHING SUGGESTIONS:

1. Students should hear this numerous times before they perform. Ask: "How many times do you hear 'G A?'" Then sing the melody emphasizing "G A" each time. Then have them play the "G A" while you sing the entirety again. Then add playing the "6 beat B," etc. Continue to add parts, while you sing the entirety.
2. Take a few special players you have and teach them the bongo and clave parts; the whole group can try the bass part.
3. "Scarf dancers" move "smoothly" in the **A** section in a circle, move with "jerky" movements in the **B** section in free space.

Jim Solomon

Author, clinician, and National Board Certified Teacher, Jim Solomon teaches classroom music and movement to grades K-5 at R. B. Hunt Elementary School in St. Augustine, Florida. There, he also directs the percussion ensemble "D.R.U.M.," the Orff Instrumental Group, Chorus, and Recorder Club.

Mr. Solomon has been recognized as the St. John's County "Teacher of the Year." He has taught Orff Schulwerk teacher training courses at many locations since 1985, including the Eastman School of Music in Rochester, New York.

The author of seven publications, Mr. Solomon has also produced a video entitled *Congas, Bongos & Other Percussion – A Guide to Technique*, an eighty-minute guide to classroom percussion instruments. He has presented at numerous National Music Conferences and workshops throughout North America.